Hey Ms. Becku

Thanks for
me. I really ho[pe you]
enjoy this book.
Much love. ♡

Jeron SANTOS

8/9/18

REBUILDING
THE TEMPLE OF
JEREMIAH

jerm davitos

Rebuilding the Temple of Jeremiah.
Copyright © 2018 by Jerm Davitos
All rights reserved under international and Pan American Copyright Conventions. Published in the United States by Lyrikah Publishing Co. No part of this book maybe reproduced in any manner whatsoever without written permission except in the case of brief quotations embodied in critical articles and reviews. For more information address www.lyrikah.com

Illustrations and Cover Design Copyrighted

First Edition
Lyrikah Publishing Co.

ISBN: 13: 978-0-692-11205-2
ISBN-10: 0-692-11205-7

In a coma…

Me: I once carried something precious with me until I didn't want it anymore. I was supposed to let success be my reason to continue walking in growth. I took those pills because of a repeated moment that would occur many more times. I'll admit I'm tired of the forced ride. It's very unfortunate my only time to make peace is now because I know I have to wake up. I know it. I never knew mama's sink or swim talk would be the waters I must SINK or SWIM in. God, I know how people want me to think you feel. I just want to know can you feel what I feel, how I feel, and possibly forgive me. I know it's a lot to ask for. I just need to know does the pain or survivor tell the story?

> God: Son, let's hike these mental mountains because I need you to do something for me.

You: God, God, God, where are you? Where am I? What am I to do?

> God: Answer your calling. Your life is a poem, you've written many. Write this one for me. You'll know the words when you listen.

emerging

rebuilding
the temple of
jeremiah

Jerm Davitos

I'm not Sorry

"They died and took your secret. I am alive I will tell your secret."

I apologize to my life.

I let this illness allow
Death as a happy place.

I let depression break me
For the times schizophrenia
Couldn't rape me.

I let anxiety cut me
For the time, my personality
Disorder couldn't rip me apart.

I gave my body up to the best
Illness, trickin' my heart in
Replacement for aching.

I got too much regret not to tell
This secret.

Illnesses are real,
But I'm the one God created.

Rebuilding the Temple of Jeremiah

Silence says things

Silence is the little boy
That plays in trees
Talks to the sky
Sleeps in his thoughts.

He calls his mother Death.
His sister Bipolar.
Him Silence.

He never knew Silence...
Rapes, pins you down,
spits emptiness
in your existence.

Sticks his manhood in a place so degrading,
you couldn't unscrew happiness from hell.

He sticks his manhood in a place
Where you stop answering to
your birth name and no one
really knows what you want
to be called.

Until you attempt to make
Your name, the way you plan
To leave this earth... suicide.

Silence says things silence
Can hear but won't repeat.

Silence wants to live like
Bright stars,
A radiant sun,
A fulfilled son,
A supportive brother.

"I've never wanted to make
Anyone happy including myself."

"I want to smile because I accomplished
Living my life, not ending it."

I want to be Jeremiah again.

Rebuilding the Temple of Jeremiah

The soil that knows the Cattleya Orchid(Me)

I bloom best in my poems
Teach me how to live in a phrase
"You're not good enough"
Teach me how to live in this phrase
And I'll show I'm somehow more than enough.
Attach me to adversity I will make it home
Neglect me my rights to be beautiful as I am
Beauty still shines when eyes are dark,
Intentions are dark,
Envy is dark.

I bloom best in my poems but I'll never know
where I could bloom next,

If I never know what else I'm good at.

~Confessions of the Cattleya Orchid(Me)
.

The Ink of a Crying Male Poet

Sincerely the Ink of a Crying Male Poet,

Ambition to write doesn't look right,
The daily whippings and reminder of why I'm a poet doesn't feel right.

I tie my faith and these poems like Bantu knots around my tomorrow.

Although tomorrow isn't promised today I didn't live in peace.

I live crying because the poems on me that are known to you as hunger pains, suicide attempts, insecurity, and dreads, are the only thing I can toast with

I still hear you laughing because a male poet looks funny.

Rebuilding the Temple of Jeremiah

I got poems written in places hieroglyphics would develop ADHD because they couldn't sit and stay.

Sit and stay
Sit and
Stay
Poems building foundations on my heart, where hurt is engraved with laughter because I'm a male poet.

I got record of what a male poet is and I'm okay, to inspire a land, rethink a nation, and change this world.

The Ink of a crying male poet doesn't bleed uselessly, it bleeds knowing the injustice will get justice one day, one day.

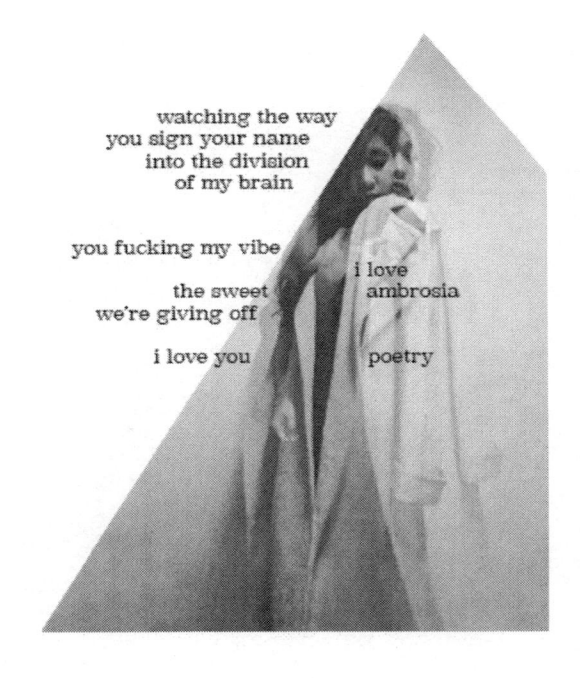

watching the way
you sign your name
into the division
of my brain

you fucking my vibe
                           i love
    the sweet   ambrosia
we're giving off

    i love you   poetry

Rebuilding the Temple of Jeremiah

Who I am

I am the last tear shed
Vaporized before hitting the ground
I am the poet
Who thought he could be poetry
I am the last tear shed.

I am distinct shattered pieces of a mirror
Crippled and crooked in reflection
Because of bullying
Because of silence
Because of because of
I am distinct shattered pieces.

I am Innocence not defined by this body
These lips I seal with silence.

I am David I can't live in this diagnosis
I'm the diagnosed.

I am Jeremiah I can't win even if I decide to lose
I'm so tired of trying to be me all day.

Let all of me flow out like streams
Different veins
We are significant.

There is We in I
"I was diagnosed with everything from schizophrenia to multiple personality disorder" -Darrell Hammonds

I'm overthinking things.
I'm under thinking things.
I'm not thinking.
I thought about it.
I'll think about it tomorrow.
I'll think if you just keep quiet.
I won't think.

Can you stitch pieces of glass?
To make a mirror?

I need to finish this poem,
But what poet is trying to write?

None of them because memories
Dimming lights like nightmares
Hearts fluttering impacted by
Destruction of depression.

Because of being misunderstood
I know everyone should understand.
I won't speak, we won't speak because
We are trying to write.

My tears falling like innocent angels,
Sacrificing their halo's or innocence
Because perfection doesn't define
These tears.

Rebuilding the Temple of Jeremiah

If I could tell you who I was
I wouldn't, because you probably
Wouldn't call me by my name.

"What you are going through, is suffering
whether you remember it or not, You're
teaching someone else to survive."

Soon I will go back and change every "I"
To "we" because There is an us in the
individual
There is opportunity for someone else's survival
in my struggle

The oneness of man and illness

I dig up the past to be the future
I live the present in seven phases
Seven perspectives
Seven objectives
Seven.

I rear in the knowledge before I fall
As my resilience picks me up
I embrace the beings
As I train the beings
With this bright future, I keep seeing.

I rage the nature of this illness
I slave to this illness
Out of the same mouth I won't praise this
illness.

I hear the oneness calling forth peace
I feel the oneness strumming my heart
I see the oneness right in arms reach to grasp
I taste the oneness as it tastes my ambition
I smell the oneness as we smell the same love.

Hear the peace
Feel my heart
See what's in reach
Taste the ambition
And smell the love

the oneness of man and illness.

Rebuilding the Temple of Jeremiah

Strong Individual

I exist with the clench of his fist
Around his pen.

I die when he finds his
Will to live.

I can be as ambitious as his mission to
overcome.

As phenomenal as I am in
Disrupting lives', I see this is a
strong individual.

Seven Writers

"I have cross the horizon to find you" –
Moana (Know who you are)

I am seven writers.
I am seven fighters.
I am seven survivors.

I tug and hug at who wants to manifest
I dive in and wash up in emotions times 7
I just know "the race is given to the one who
Endures
it until the end."

I could not live with seven demonic angels.
I could not bow down to seven troubled points
in history.
I could not.

I was labeled at an early age
My future had already been made.

I remember being at the E.R. and she asked my
diagnosis…
As I give my long drawn out list of pills.
I paused because I was discouraged to say I'm
mentally ill.

Rebuilding the Temple of Jeremiah

When you multiply trauma, divide it by
abandonment, add depression, and subtract
hope.
You have the ugly truth, the revelation,
the bitter frustration.

I gather the origins of sanity, the yin
 and yang for adversity,

The pen and paper...
So, I write, we write
I fight, no we fight
My God is bigger than this
I'm destined to survive.

"It will work out for the good of them"
Says the creator.

Why hide the imperfect beauty?
Why feel insecure about the truth?
Why?

Risking

Just for peace of mind
I dig trenches in my history
I began writing

I beg the world around me...
"Wind stop howling like depressed wolves
Clouds stop crying like your purpose is unsure."

I reopen the wounds and listen to their story
I remove bandages, cast, crutches, lies, and people.
Anything to unwarp the memory of the true history
And the past comes to me spelling freedom in a phrase

"Open this generation's eyes"
I open the past and what it says is profound
"Risking peace for the truth,
is seeing the risk needed to be taken is making the truth peaceful"

I hope it can be.

Rebuilding the Temple of Jeremiah

It's Days Like This

It's days when I am tired of trying to make the
world understand me
Understand that I'm scared of suicide, but I
hate being alive.

In this world ain't no compromise for me
Ain't no freedom, sanity, none of that.

I don't see a future
I see hell on its way.

I'm tired of fighting
It ain't surviving because I am suffering.

Made mockery of by family.
Can't go and get, everything handed to me.

I don't see tears as sunshine following
Tears just a reminder that I am defeated
Just have to manage because I'm afraid of
dying.

It's days like this where I
Just want to crawl back up
Into God's last thought
And be unthought-of

I haven't seen his purpose for me
And I have felt nothing but insecurity.

i trust your hands
patting my back, better
than your promises in the bible

im a sinner religously,
but i am a creation in
your mind, before i
breathe sucess and
exhale faliure

god, share your poetic
thoughts with my
essence, my universe

detect my hidden
rivers somwhere in my
eyes... ifound just
comfort in
silence,
please.

we will make it
to the new found
land of milky
soft depression and
smooooth
chasing anxiety

we are not metaphors
.... sometimes

Rebuilding the Temple of Jeremiah

                                                    I'm Here

Whether the days are long
Nights are short
I'm right here giving my support.

I've never loved someone to love myself.
I've never loved myself to love someone.

                              I sway, they're lost

Once we existed in their existence

Treated like pennies on the ground

I had to appreciate my worth, and become
stingy about who I spend my confidence on

So now I sway, and they're lost

I sway 'wayyyyyy' back like the wings of birds I
extend to catch my wind

I sway down low like I loan my confidence to
someone conceited but I extend my worth so
I'm high priced in my spirit

I swing my resilience through that fast-
revolving door and clock in at Now'0'clock

And I spread my sway like clouds dripping tears
of potential, drizzling ambition, and pouring
down these poems

I sway in a way they don't understand, and
they're lost

Rebuilding the Temple of Jeremiah

Fly

Be over the things that
Tries to contain you
Retain you
And strain you.

Become a tower of resilience
Never stay down
Always rebuild
and never not forgive yourself.

Fly and scrap the mountains to catch air
Ride the winds
As they bring you to overcome your struggles.

Don't worry about the things beneath you
They are there to stall you
Just fly.

Take a trip to a place of peace
That is destined within
Your own essence.

I reach out to you with my heart
Grab ahold of the love you need
To prosper in this lonesome world.

I know you're afraid
But don't be.

Be fierce stand with pride
Fly towards your dream
Not your destiny.

Fly Where My Wings Guide Me

I was working on a tribute poem for Mr.
Moody Black I couldn't start because his impact
as a male poet awes me so much I could not
resist but to write about how it made me feel.
Mr. Black has played multiple phenomenal roles
in my life. He showed me "BE A MAN AND
A POET". No one can dim your light unless
you reveal the circuit. I love the way he carries
himself while also being humble through great
success.

I wrote a poem called "Fly Where my Wings
Guide Me" inspired by Mr. Moody Black.

Riding on the wind of judgement,
Sipping on sunset waiting to devour sunrise

Posture not fetal,
Wings not tucked,
Fears not acknowledged,
Ambitions arched like
Crowning dreams to be born.

I'm too much of a poet not to be one.
I'm less of a forced dreamed.
Because the way my pen bribed me
I fly where these wings guide me.

Having visions of dreams
long before man knew I'd fulfill them.

Rebuilding the Temple of Jeremiah

Beckoning silence as it shatters my teeth
because my voice sings.

Watch me whip adversity.

Write seas down to oceans
and oceans down to rivers.

Write some hope in the lost,
and find what's lost in the found.

Tears flowing in because
I can be a man and a poet.

Black like the night sky my ink dries
and shines bright like the poetry on my heart.

I got confirmation I can be just me.
A man like the man GOD created me to be.

Don't believe me just watch.

My posture not fetal.
Wings not tucked.
Fears not acknowledged.
Ambitions arched like
Crowning dreams.

I'm too much of a poet not to be one.

no. i didnt fall

i landed
where
god
wanted
me to
land

Rebuilding the Temple of Jeremiah

Depression Get Back

Feelings of sadness, useless, and hopelessness
Anger, irritation, over pointless things
Loss of will to live
The growth in appetite.

Racing thoughts.
Tired body.
Lack of concentration.
Focus on suicide.

I give you a name, I call you by name
Depression get back.

Go back to your depressed mind.
Depression lose your will to live.
Commit suicide I don't care
But
Don't hold your burdens over my head.

Leave my nation of thoughts alone.
Leave my existence alone.
Leave my purpose alone.

If you don't
My thoughts must stand together
Making a pledge to my hand
Write, write, write
A promise to the words speak, speak, speak
GET BACK before I write, speak, and tell you
the truth.

Daily Doses of Remembrance

Would I rather have weight gain or mental
pain?
Would I rather learn to love me or let the world
kill me?
I take Prozac and Abilify every day to unlearn
the beatings of silence
To feel the beatings of silence
To not heal from the beatings of silence

When I was little, a rock in my eye wasn't
enough to prepare me for blows ahead
E.R. Visits for asthma attacks weren't enough
to prepare me for wanting to lose my life
Friends weren't friend enough to tell me they
could easily become enemies and bullies

I sang silence favorite note in a choir of secrets
I felt pain's heavenly hell while trying
to regurgitate swallowed rage
Feeling I was bulimic in my spirit I tried to
regurgitate my own physical existence

Daily doses remind me I surf on waves of
depression like plants bathe in sun
Bent and bruised like water in a faucet
Hiding in my own absence only made me
present for suicides role call

They remind me what doesn't kill you makes
you wonder why it didn't
They remind me what I forget to remember

Rebuilding the Temple of Jeremiah

While praising remembrance of the hole in my throat

Daily doses remind me...
Silence will kill you for not speaking
Speaking will heal you for not kissing the delicious lips of silence

I'm a mental health patient
Everyday I'm reminded why I should have given up
I want to be remembered for the reason I didn't.

Rebuilding the Temple of Jeremiah

when will my dying leaf mean
something to a blooming tree

i know i made her
feel beautiful last year

ive fallen and she lives on and
loves on without me

Crisis

I got up and jumped into my deepest thoughts
And I fell endlessly to until I hit rock-bottom

I rode my wave of emotions
And I got caught in the spiral

I lit a match in the darkness
But the wind whirled in cursive
"freedom doesn't exist here"

Tried signing over my rights
My feelings loved attacking me too much

Rebuilding the Temple of Jeremiah

Broken existence, speak your existence

I broke both hands trying to carry both your world and my own

I clinched my truth so I could accommodate your fantasy

I now only have these full lips that begs me to speak... The truth, the truth, the truth

-Signed a boy who won't please his depression

Bipolar, Depression, etc.

Don't get me wrong the illness is real
But on my rock bottom days
This illness will not destroy my will to live

It will not destroy the message attached to my existence
I don't reside in any diagnosis
I don't breathe medication
I bind my purpose and passion and I begin my meditation

I pray that those clouds inspire me harder than depression saddens me
I strive harder than any emotions desire to dominate my intelligence

I recollect a time that I thought my future was nothing more than a grave site
I recollect a time that I tried but no tear would fall from my eyes

It was in that moment I knew Bipolar, Depression, Etc. Was not for me or you

So, keep fighting!

Rebuilding the Temple of Jeremiah

A Resilient Accident

"I wrote this for a bully who had no remorse for what they had done..."

What was meant to kill and break me only made me.

I been seasoned in words and names I didn't know I was to answer to.

So much love put into making me hate myself.

Clicking pens on the horizon of insanity.

Spicing up my will to die, so when I do to a bully it would be so sweet.

Mixing anger with sips and shots of hope.

Vengeance tasting like a flavor I should never again produce.

Forgiveness smelling like a chance to dive out of the seas of depression.

I call all my friends who have been bullied to the table.

Their recipe to destroy us only turned us into a dish they will always hate.

Suicide may be in the mind of the one planning a homicide.

You created a vision for me to see my resilience.

You probably hate it was an accident.

Rebuilding the Temple of Jeremiah

INK

I wrote a poem for my relief
I write a song because nobody else's
Lyrics I knew how to sing
I bled blue, black, and pink

Teasing Tattoos because I have words
Already engraved on my heart

I bled the ink of a poet

Those words holding my heart together are...

"You must love again to heal."

Example of Being Humble-

thank you to hard times you
were more friend to me than I was to you.

You let me dwell which is something I'd love if
I knew how to give up.

I'll always know what you're capable of.

I know what I'm capable of as well.

Hard Times being the stroke that
tries time after time to cripple my walk, faith,
and dream.

I'm humbled because you inspire me to be as
ambitious as you are.

As focused as you are.

As considerate as you are of others.

I just choose to do mine differently.

Rebuilding the Temple of Jeremiah

Lost in the Sea

There's times when depression finds me

Devours me

Because it envies me.

I let it.

Trying to prevail in a literal hell you
can't tell me I'm not lost in his sea.

You won't tell me that I'm worth living.

You won't tell me I'll live through this if its
killing me.

I know I'm lost in the sea, the sea where hope has drowned,
and faith is the key, where's the door in an entire sea?

I cannot fathom land where hands are dry
Hands can write.

The sharp, violating, and horny touch of depression
attempting to arouse me, guides to a place where my mind says, "suicide is okay."

Depression putting his genitalia in a place I refuse to be
 fucked because my happiness is mine and dammit it's time.

I thrive. This sick bastard that has touched the little boy I was,
fucked my teenage years, I'll be damned if it ends my life.

I may be lost at sea but...

Faith is a key that unlocks unseen doors.

Faith is a key.

Tribute to Jaylani Phommachanh

Rebuilding the Temple of Jeremiah

He loves me and I hate him

I've never been sexually abused but…

Touch me Just Not There

I never just considered myself homosexual

Until I knew the one thing loving me right was dominant
, masculine, strong in the mind, is a manlike experience.

What straight man gets aroused by the rubbing, touching,
 lust, performance of a man like experience?

Sometimes when he walks in my mind he slams me to the ground

Pins me down and makes me love his will and purpose.

He whips out his psychotic vibes and it turns me on   …

maybe even into a beast.

I never just considered myself a homosexual.

The way he loves on me and violates me when
 I am happy I struggle to want to
know the power of a woman.

I rub on his size 12 making myself the
fill in on the depressions in his shoe.

I lick between his mouth and thoughts
at times, I can't utter my own.

We rock and grind between night and day
trying to prove our resilience is stronger
than our attachment to each other.

If he loves me so hard, but deep down
I hate him is this an abusive relationship?

If he comforts me when nothing else can,
 can he be a knight in shining armor to another
man?   ...

Rebuilding the Temple of Jeremiah

If he really loves me and I really hate him can
we cut strings like suicide kills or a comas sleep?

If I really hate him why did I let
him touch me at the age of 9?

Why didn't I tell mama his name?

.. now I must carry him around because
his sex game on my mind at times
I don't know how to part with.

Why didn't I just tell mama his name?
Why didn't I?
Why?

Mama would've made him go away?
Could she have killed him?

You can't kill a man you can't see,
and if she attempts she'd be killing all of me.

Mama if I tell you his name is Schizophrenia
what can you do to help me?

I'm stuck.

Perspective of David the Doctor...
All About Me Poem: You mean us?

Everyone has an agent Patty who helps organize their mind.

Everyone has an Innocence and her silence is guilty.

Everyone has a Depression that makes beautiful dreams smell like poisoned baked cookies.

Everyone has a man who is a shadow because he lost himself.

Everyone has a moment they want to shine.

Silence is the one that sings "oh happy day."

When winds whisper everyone has a conscious that watts away mosquitoes that loves the resilience in our veins…

Rebuilding the Temple of Jeremiah

Everyone will always want to shine.

What about when you can't?
What about when your purpose is secular to the
main purpose?
What about this poem being about one person,
yet many bombards to make their statements
law in what must exist?

What about the hurt you can control?

Jeremiah got high tonight and wrote this why
isn't this about him.

IT FEELS REAL GOOD
TO LET GO
LIKE FLAMES
IN THE AIR

Rebuilding the Temple of Jeremiah

The Moment That Hurt Us Most

Praying to God as if he shows favoritism,

I can't persuade myself that I'm special and my hurt is greater than anyone's.

Suicide knows the conversations we've had.

We chalk out the image of our sacrifice to survive in this life and we chant our impurities to God.

We light our own candles because we hope to finally have created something meaningful in the darkness.

We too often sacrifice happiness just too live and live pain.

The time we didn't sacrifice our life to understand the happiness in death.

We pray we fathom some meaning. Our pain is understood. Etch these survival instincts on the one who wants to live.

It's the one that wants to die that survives best.

Suicide committing crimes, yet to be arrested.

Harassing me every day, I've always wanted to die I guess I'll have to survive best.

The moment that hurt us most...

Is living when at times death is more appealing.

S. E. P. T- Sexual Experiences Penetrating Time

"Can we make up for the eternity we can't spend together?" - Silence

I just love the way he grips my universe.
Caress my every ambition for one night.

He touches my high as I hit his blunt.
Then our intentions are blunt.

Let's make love alive.

Let's make love alive.
The way you lick on me makes my erection comes closer, and you whisper, "come closer."

The way you embrace this mind game
We both can't survive
There's only one winner.

And I want to make love alive.

Let's make love alive.

You can call me big daddy.
Right now, I don't want to be cute or sexy.

Let me dig in you intertwine my tricks in the veins of your spirit.

Let's bind our eternal beings but I plan to win.
So, let's make love alive.

Let me put these feelings in you so you can remember you're only a moment.

Let me pull your hair grab your neck and make you bend for me.

The other night I almost bent for you.
But, I like making love alive.

Let's take a break and sip some praises in this room because I didn't wrap it up.

I also want this feeling to keep me alive, When I fucked suicide and played with his mind.

I never liked you, I'm just a player you taught me well.

Rebuilding the Temple of Jeremiah

Are you a legend?

A legend (me) never heard the story of another legend (mental illness) and said, " I want to be like them."

A legend finds the story worth surviving and lives legendarily.

How to be phenomenal.

It's not about the success.
It's about your endurance through failure.
It's about your endurance period.

Rebuilding the Temple of Jeremiah

Depression
You will rise up to be the man God wants you
to be.
I will stiff your walk throughout life.
It will come as a scare that I might appear to be
more loyal than the gods,
More resilient than Prozac, Risperdal, or Abilify.
I will see to it that you rise up to be the man
God wants you to be.

About What I(Depression) Expects

Don't put the scars on you.
Beat them into the memories,
When no one could rock your tears,
Clothe your pain,
Feed your aspiration,
Amplify your voice,
You cry black tears.

Rebuilding the Temple of Jeremiah

What I Will Do to You
You will write a way for no way.
You speak with intimidation.
But...
You walk with confidence
That life won't snatch you
By those twist and drag you,
Steal from you,
Peel your skin,
Pour bleach on your flesh,
Stitch it all back up making...
You...
Remember...
It can and will happen again.

                              I'm Very Perverted
The sexiness in your intellect I prey on like the
wolf does the sheep.
I'm on the hunt to devour your- up-bringing.
I dig my hurt in your eyes through watching
your family fall apart.

Rebuilding the Temple of Jeremiah

                                  So… Perverted…
I dig my hurt in your eyes through watching
your mother
Fight to live but she doesn't get an extra day, no
one does.
Look at your sister leave. She can't seem to
realize reality doesn't
Spoon feed a fantasy.

                              I'm Your God
I hear you cry for your god and I always say,
I AM HERE.
I hear you pray for someone and I always
assure,
I AM HERE.
You dwell in hope that you've been given what
you deserve so,
I AM HERE.

Rebuilding the Temple of Jeremiah

                                        The Irony

I believe in the idiot I am.
The idiot you are, because you didn't believe the idiot in me.

                                        Sincerely,
I gave you this piece
I let you disobey me
So, write because the end of this I will be
waiting.
Do you like me, your Depression?

Rebuilding the Temple of Jeremiah

                                        I was winded

A crooked arch starting at the hook of my tears
Finding there was no tear sharper than this one

The next tear was a dried scar
Where I was cut to the core

No life deserved a great disrespect as this

I ran after my life because it was the reason I existed
I fell, and I was winded from these winds of disturbing hatred

I did not know I'd live the rest of my life winded
Jabs in gut
Pain signals stabbing heart

I curled at a point in life I was supposed to stand tall.

                              In the closet
Hiding in the storage boxes
Behind clothes
In the pockets where loose change
Would soon be treasure

Stuck in the cobwebs
I could not free myself
From the threads, of
what life had stitched me to

I was in this closet
Schizophrenia was just waiting to wear me.

Rebuilding the Temple of Jeremiah

　　　　　　　　　　　　Translucent memories

Smiling
Laughing
Jokes

I saw right through you
I went straight to the front door
To the man that wouldn't let me leave

I asked him why does he follow me?
At night, why does he call for me?
Why do he look so scary?

One day he answered but I had to swear not to tell.

                                I went off

I splash in pain
I'm soaked in silence
Down in the backyard trees
I destroyed the branches
Like broken memories

I uproot the trees
Like the secrets, I'm hiding

I lied about what happened to the trees
Like the truth, I was despising.

Rebuilding the Temple of Jeremiah

My thoughts to God

I'm only supplied with nothing
These facets of the life I want to live
I'm full of tired
Because I can't see the light
Because I can't see the reason to fight

I'm empty on forgiveness
Because I can't forgive myself
Because I can't forgive silence
For talking while I tried and waited
and waited and tried to speak

I have so much to say
Just give me the words
Give me the perfect pronunciation
And I promise I will come clean
About the darkness inside of me

Dear God,
        Please listen.
                Sincerely,
                      A drifting heart

                    Is it too late?

I tried to keep quiet
The resistance didn't work with me

Quietness broke
Once I broke the string
Resistance wrapped around me
Choking me graciously

I see shadows in the shadows
I see night in the day
I hear a crowed in the silence
I hear the crowd coming my way
I smell silence approaching to shut me up

Not anymore.

I have scars on my skin where I tried to eat
To suppress these angelic demons
I have holes in my trust where I thought silence
Would speak

Please tell me
Is it too late?

Mama?

Rebuilding the Temple of Jeremiah

1/7

Hidden in the mind of exploration
I found myself loving
I found myself dividing
I found myself loving the division

Am I the dominant being?
I mean I love this skin I'm in
Is this the being God created to prosper?

Healing Wounds

Epigraph-
Living life shedding tears as if they compensate. My dark room, my broken dedications, I dedicate this poem to a group wanting to survive, trying to survive, willing to learn how to survive, when the mind doesn't. — This is from my Depression Journal on a day I was inspired.

They can't mend our scars, so we tell special stories.
Stories about night we are bent over the lap of insomnia.

Assess spanked but we want rest, we need rest.
We pray, we come together.

Everybody suffers something, so we gather like this & we confess our scars because they won't let us sleep.

If they won't let us sleep, we can't let them heal.

Crossed out on the cross, I understand why some lay down their life.

Rebuilding the Temple of Jeremiah

So, pain can unwarp of pure memories.

We need to see the vision of survival.
I want we, us, I, you know our struggle is
another's survival.
Let's join like choirs, singing survival instincts.
Let us pray this pen and paper our God gave us
rock us like lullabies, into comas of resilience.
Let's us dance leaving our footprints on the
head of depression.
Depression has taken lives to survive
We must take depression and learn to live,

Revive the fallen,
Inspire the broken,
We all are broken,

It's time we heal.

In unison let's say amen together…
1,2,3… Amen

Deep Purple Depression
I see purple as a flame of loyalty.

Like fiery embers solitude ascends,
Trespassing into the playground of
Emptiness.

I swear I've written for colored beings a lot.

I wish to see a white dove lacking pigment of
loyalty,
But transcending peace like smoked from a
loved cigar.

As I right to the mountains,
And left with proof, only thing loyal is
depression.

Am I the wrong presence, and maybe the right
absence?
These confessions are purple to a dove.

These hopes are eager for peace.

Signed with invisible ink.

God, Passively Rock Me in Your Arms...
When I was thought of by you it was evident I would need you. I need purpose like candles need flames. I want to be caught by your eye, baptized in your tears, because we both cry the struggle of being loved. I want you, God to carry me in your blessings. I prayed you caress my wondering heart, and with each stroke you answer the questions I need answered most. Do I? Do I? God, do I do your will in a way I deserve to feel the warmth of your arms? Do I mend my purpose to excel the calling of what I am here for? God, I call out to you because this is more than a praise poem, this is my essence poem. This is my praise, I am my poem. God write me with your perfect pen and sway my purpose. Sign me as a blessing to another life, God I need purpose...
God passively rock me in your arms, I'm aggressively in need.

This is for Jatavious Addison: Burgundy Scrubs

I would like to honor a friend, a family, and hopefulness. - The words of Resilience

I know where you are and where you are going.

To a place you don't know.

I see hugs comfort like hope is abundant.

We travel places unimaginable in our minds where reality leaves us at the door.

Burgundy scrubs signal a farewell with hope to meet the old you again.

I promise I know you're scared and I wish there was a length of time we could pass to heal your wounds.

I know what those burgundy scrubs mean.

Rebuilding the Temple of Jeremiah

I pray, prayers carry you like the wings of birds.

I pray that the Lord hems your scars and
straightens your pain.
I pray the devil get his medicine back on him.

I pray God has the last say so.

I pray God will have a say so.

I know what those burgundy scrubs mean.

I know the resilience in you is going to awaken
and I pray

Those burgundy scrubs detach from your skin

Like freedom rings.

Those scrubs are not your skin...

Let your freedom ring.
Let your freedom ring.
Jatavious let your freedom ring.

Dear Brother,

"I want to be like you so bad" -My Brother

Your ability to make the ones around you feel special is extraordinary.
Your willingness to go without so others can go with has done more than inspired me.
You know, I once heard "when life gives you lemons… just smile anyway."
You do just that.
I have a question, a few actually…
How do you smile through troubling times?
What do you get from a friendship like ours?
Do you ever feel lonely depressed?
About that last question, if you are I am here for you.
I just wonder these things because I want to be like you.

#YouInspireMe

Rebuilding the Temple of Jeremiah

A Day I'll Get Back for The Rest Of my Life

To cherish you
To realize how true you are, my friend.

If you're my real friend.

Causing my every tear, letting them wash me away.

Thank you.

Good morning, My Inspiration

I woke up with you on my mind
It's been five years how did I lose time?

How bitter you made me feel.

My bitter inspiration I'll write until my it's known
That my hand and this pen will never detach.

I'll write you away. One day. One day.

Rebuilding the Temple of Jeremiah

I feel like.

nothing... nothing at all today

A Lesson from My Mama: There's Nothing Louder Than Silence

It takes two to argue.

Only one has to carry on… and on… and on some more.

Then the truth is revealed and that's who started it.

I'm Finna Go

Before I take a loss for my future, a victory for insanity,

Imma take it to the king, then imma visit my land of poetry

Where I am the creator of my imagination.

Holding this world of mine by the roots that might not pass the test of time.

They will trace back to a place where they sing "this little light of mine, imma let it shine."

I'm finna go to a place I call L.O.L, living outside limits.

Finna go to a place where I create a winner, so I know imma win it.

Im finna go.

I'm Gonna Write this Mental Illness Away

I am going to write this illness up out of my mind, my body, and spirit. I am gonna take a dose of this pen and paper, with this I'm hoping I'll write myself into something greater. They did their damage, they made me live their damage for a long time, but I can only see what I need to repair in myself. I know how I'll repair it too. Let this pen and paper be my foundation. On this foundation I will construct of place of refuge. This depression, these voices, and these personalities not going to hold me back from a calling that'll preserve the life of someone special. Pills will no longer be popped with the seeking of satisfaction, because this pen and paper is my foundation. God gave me the wisdom to know the things I can change, he also gave me the strength to change. Mama showed me pen and paper has done more healing than a doctor, and I forever thankful. Resilient I am, a warrior I am, a survivor I am, a beautiful struggle I am, an inspiration to myself I will always be. I am going to degrade this illness the same exact way it repeatedly degraded me. I am my opportunity for my new beginning. I will have a victory over this battle, someday, one day, real… real… soon. Depression has taken everything… taken everything from me except my faith, pen, and paper. With these three survivors I will prosper, I will survive. This mental illness has caged me from opportunities, friends, family, made me feel useless to the point I felt didn't deserve to

Rebuilding the Temple of Jeremiah

live or shed a hurting tear. But oh, how this pen and paper brought restoration to my existence. I am working on living a new life, inspired and a positive viewing on life.

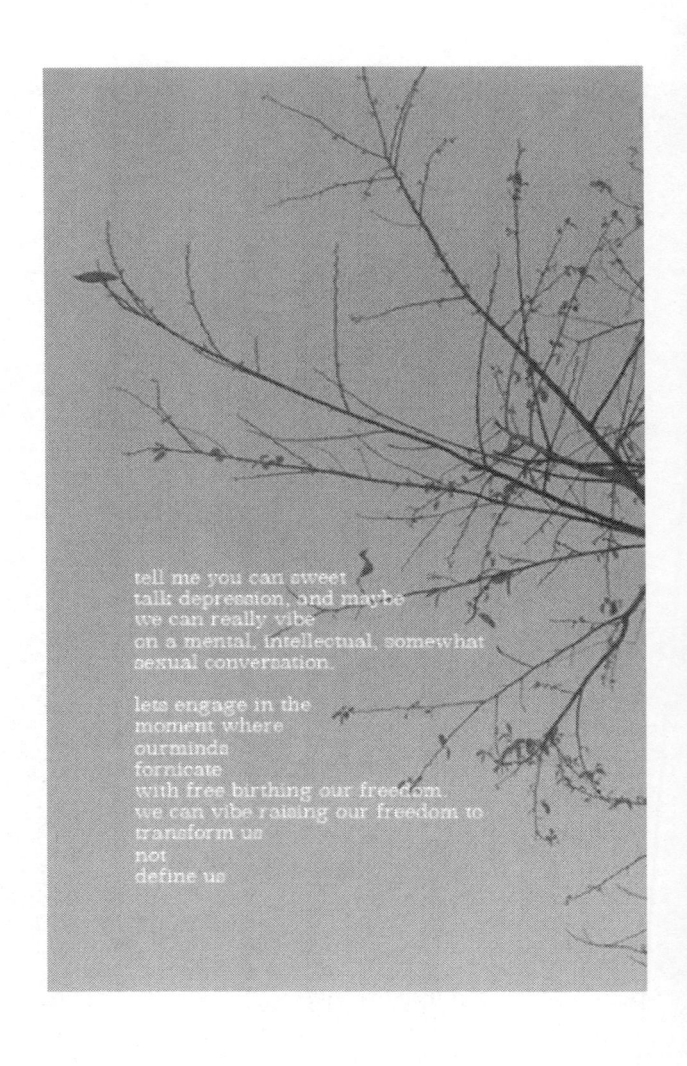

tell me you can sweet
talk depression, and maybe
we can really vibe
on a mental, intellectual, somewhat
sexual conversation.

lets engage in the
moment where
ourminds
fornicate
with free birthing our freedom.
we can vibe raising our freedom to
transform us
not
define us

Rebuilding the Temple of Jeremiah

daily photos
to capture
gods poetry

my healing

You're My Smooth Cocaine... I'm So Functional with You in Me

My thoughts map out like the united states,
 but they never come together just like the
united states.

I went from loving you
twenty-four seven to giving myself better than
you.

We are dysfunctional,
very dysfunctional at times,
can we function enough to sing...?
 a gospel song?

One more thing...

Tumble like thorns,
Into the skin,
Blistering,
Bruising,
Life through,
And like memories.

It Does Not Matter If a Real Experience Does Not Occur

Dear Depression,

If you touch my DNA distortedly
I'll show you Resilience's wrath.
Do love me knowing there's a cost, and it
doesn't matter.
Love me if it doesn't hurt you,
or leaves you bed ridden
to the road that makes you
hated.

The trees have cut their alliance to nature
because nature loves her Bipolar too much.
I'm on Nature's side and I'm hurting too so I
am not ready to heal, yet.

Rebuilding the Temple of Jeremiah

I Don't Need Family, I Don't Need to Be Gay

Mama I don't have to be your son,
Dad I can't disappoint you a second time,
Grandma I don't have to be your grandson,
Uncles I never was your nephew,
Depression loves me,
My fish and hermit crabs are all I could hope to
really love me,
Come hell out of the ground I don't have
anything.
I need wind, I'm tired.

I'm loving the honest poetry, I hope it loves me
back.

On the DL

Depression…
Loves me.

2/24/18

Rebuilding the Temple of Jeremiah

COMA

Coming to realize
Only imagination that saves
Me, Is the day I
Expire

On to another
Niche that needs me.

One day when I am ready to really die, I hope my absence is worth a little more than my presence.
2/24/18

Rebuilding the Temple of Jeremiah

Whatever's wrong with me, is a bitch
I'm a suicidal person who doesn't wanna die.
I'm negative.
I don't belong.
Pain is like stitches designed for my existence.
This is not an experience, this is life.
Just let me enjoy the long forgotten, how long
fall, just care a little, not too much.
God hold me tight.

Don't Try to Understand

Don't try to understand
Amen is a great part of the lie you're telling
Some try to underestimate this power and all of
a sudden amen to stay away
Tried writing prose to prepare for pain
It's a mass that's goes deep into the mind
murdering innocence, 'foeva'
Depression just erected his semen on my chest
Peace be patient
Be grateful you have something
Depression is here like I prayed one million
times for it
I house depression, yet he never thanks me or
says he loves me
Keep ya tools in ya pants I don't wanna look
gay or feminine to everyone
Think about condoms or being considerate
sometimes please!

Rebuilding the Temple of Jeremiah

How can a man be a man if he doesn't cry?

I'm going crazy today.

A Long Poem with Little Meaning

Ripples in time
Lapsing in hearts
Attacking the aura
of peace and humility,

does it
always
have to be
about
you.

Held captive is the heart

and

Rebuilding the Temple of Jeremiah

The heart holds   love captive
and love hinders a breakthrough

forcing positive or negative
change to never happen…

foeva

I

I took my mind to the doctor, they said I need
breaks on my breaking points, they say I need
new resilience because I am rolling on four flats,
And I said

AMEN, I fucking agree

Rebuilding the Temple of Jeremiah

HUH?

Your logic to solving magic is making magic
happen in my mind, I love you too.

The center of oblivion is hiking its only
question…

What am I?

Rebuilding the Temple of Jeremiah

Rage has lost its opportunity to process pain.

I confess I promised once upon a time I'd make depression smile, hoping it would make us both happy.

It never made a difference in my heart.

At least I tried, I wish I hadn't.

Rebuilding the Temple of Jeremiah

Chief

Command my rage with your embrace, only your embrace.

Compose my tears with your smile.

My family in my head is so 'depressfunctional'

can you just battle my flaws, they love your fight?

Rebuilding the Temple of Jeremiah

What if I could be
a dying flower,
symbolic for a new season,
not lack of care?

Depression is my wife, fucking me like a husband,

I'd be lying if I deny my walk with a limp at times.

Rebuilding the Temple of Jeremiah

Hey You

Meditate my mind into your balance, because
my body 'gratitified' with whips and names
tattooed on me are the things I would die for,
last night.

I'd be lying if I said I hated pain in certain
places, like my ego, my pride, my contributions
to my success. what if I just tell the truth?

My Family Forgets

It's not how "masculine" I am it's how
inextinguishable my heart is in the face of
depression and still survived what was taken.
I've cut myself with horrific lines and I am
ashamed to bleed, and bleed, bleed something
everyone has… pain.
I'm bleeding winds, asthma attacking my verbal
prayers.

I was never programmed to fake a smile, I just
hope I can create me a real one, then someone
else a real one.

Rebuilding the Temple of Jeremiah

Yesterday I literally hanged myself with the thought

"Positive thoughts equal happiness" but I love black walls to create my own definition of paradise.

> Jeremiah, Jerm, Jerm Davitos,
> Silence, David, Mental- Kidd3,
> Youngdaviastaboy__
> I forgive you for…

1. Leaving the door open to insomnia
2. Not talking
3. Not talking
4. Not believing in you
5. Believing you
6. Trying to suppress you
7. Trying to depress you
8. For depressing you
9. Fighting tears
10. Itchy dessert dry eyes
11. Not releasing

Rebuilding the Temple of Jeremiah

    12. Not letting you be known
    13. Breaking my favorite mirror
    14. Breaking my one reflection
    15. Breaking Jeremiah
        ...
    16. Forgetting Jeremiah
    17. Trying to kill Jeremiah
    18. Killing Jeremiah
    19. Not resuscitating Jeremiah
    20. For not being sorry for so long

                      I forgive you, for you

I hope I love the vibes more than the weed.
I refuse to speak.
I simply love you,
a lot.
Hoping all can be well.
I broke my favorite mirror.
Healing the broken barrier.
I look to blame everyone else.

Rebuilding the Temple of Jeremiah

>I am my Superhero.
>I will never get this low… again

Teach me how to properly hold and care for
- Solitude

Is this the place where I turn lights off in my mind,
Light little thought candles,
And feel poetic?

Do I need to love these moments?
How do exhale who I'm trying to be, and inhale who I am?

How do I snooze my mental alarm?

Must I carry my purpose, what if I want to abort it?

When can I write a poem?

This is the place where you turn lights off in your mind,
Light little thought candles,

And feel poetic.

Love these moments.
Inhale who you are, then exhale who you're trying to be.

Carry your purpose, do not abort it.

Then, then, and only then, you write a poem.
I apologize to myself for not being a poet when I could've been, when I should've been.
I apologize to myself for not mediating the chaos between my body and mind. I could've explained each perspective more.

And

I apologize to myself for not respecting my poetic voice, and using it to hurt others.

I don't think

I don't think I am destined to make others understand, I am destined to inspire those who understand.
I am firmly grounded in work and power of Mu Kumfair.

Rebuilding the Temple of Jeremiah

													Trauma

Something or someone had convinced me I'll
burn in a hell,
but how?

I am already living on earth.

The worst, absolute worst trauma there is, is
taking me out of a situation I'm learning to
survive in.

Learning the beauty of imperfection, dried out
my desire for perfection.

               B
   my divinE
               I
               N
               G

Mu Kumfair is my balance.
To my scale he outweighs the dominance.

Mu Kumfair is blessing me depression,
Gifting me resilience,
Teaching me to inspire.

P.S. it's simply beautiful. It really is.

Rebuilding the Temple of Jeremiah

In My Distinct Mental Language

Mu Kumfair add elegance to my schizophrenic tongue
Mu Kumfair make their intake not gibberish, but praise
Mu Kumfair who I am distinct
Make what I do remind the "mental"
That I can speak every language.

				Vibezz

They are the same as energy to others.
Vibes is what I like, energy is what I make it.

The Three P's to Entitlement

Please self, make meaningful
Progress and never
Place second in being YOU.

Anxiety Attack

Breath in, breathe out. I am still human.

Rebuilding the Temple of Jeremiah

I wander
&
Wonder in
Search
For peace
.
Peace, kiss
Me
One more
Time
.
Before every
Hell
Breaks loose
.
Every hell
.

                                    #TeamWork
God if you can battle
Time.
I won't give
    Up.

Celebrity Name Poem

In a Nick of time,
I became a
Loose,
Poetic,
Cannon.

I told my imaginary friend,
Mariah,
I could no longer,
Carry
Us both.

I'm sorry.

                    Affirmation to Myself
Love me when I can't or make me love me
when I want to know why.
Love me how I cannot find love or express
(Gay?)
Your love is unique and/or angelic.
Now teach me to vibe,
In my solitude,
My…
Solitude,
My solitude.

Rebuilding the Temple of Jeremiah

                                             Wow
Wow, I've been trying to poet my revenge.
I just realized the best revenge is to live,
Swim in water,
Walk dry land,
And fly in the sky.

P.S. The most poetic moments are simple plans
to do the necessary at that time.

P.S. I love you.

Inhale Who I am.
Trap me in your embrace,
Hug me until I understand your protection.
Amaze my next poem, it's
 about you.

Swallow me whole to intake, inhale who
I am.

I love having relations that help
 me produce my identity

Rebuilding the Temple of Jeremiah

sacrificial blessings are
the blues of my life.
Playing my symphony and pain
orchestrating my heart with lungs
to love and breathe
for you

what if we could pass
these troubling times and slip
into eternal resilience?

Leaking Thoughts 2
I need to reconcile with my "what if's."
I'm too full of poetry to already be empty.
I feel the contractions of another poem…
Being birthed!!

"Birth me, I will give you strength."

Rebuilding the Temple of Jeremiah

I'm starting to get back depressed again.
I'm hearing voices again.

Abomination-
/Jer. Ra. Miyah./ Jeremiah
noun
To be created with purpose, hands, and vision, only to destroy one(self)(existence) with the same purpose, hands, and vision.
Worse than Suicide.
"Why does He create abominations and call them beautiful? I wonder, I really do."

Rebuilding the Temple of Jeremiah

      living an uncomfortable color with hope

    i found out i was never black and
dangerous
      i am bright a resilient

dear skin and perception

      im only black when i look
      inferior to privilege
      im only dangerous when i discover
      i am the key to unlock
      myself from racial incarceration
      skin, im so sorry the first thing
      you're entitled to is rejection
      we will however make them remember
      not to forget us

to my skin, i respect you down to
      the last revolution of flight
      for superiority
      you've been belittled too long
      to settle for equality on a color
      wheel that has rights
      and leaves you with imagination

as for you perception.
      i was never black
      and dangerous

Jeremiah- Depressed PrOphET

I can't hide, depression has left me naked, only
the truth to wrap myself in.
I'll preach until I reach.

In This Eternity

There's nothing in this eternity I'd wanna love
more, than the hope of another eternity with
perfection in my veins... and recollections of
imperfect and depressed poems on paper...
from the past teaching me what it means to
survive.

I am thoroughly depressed.
Severely dissociative.

Cease this broken palace of thoughts.

If I Need to Write A Suicide Note to Mama

Hi mama, as you prepare for my funeral I have a few request...
Dress me nice I want to have a nice green outfit on... designed by Freedom my imaginary stylist

Get my pair of wings out my armoire and bring them,
I want to fly after my funeral.
Get my super powers and pay the bill one more time... I want to make sure I've helped someone... anyone.

Email Halle Berry tell her to come kiss my forehead after Celine Dion sings "I'm Your Angel."
So Email Celine Dion too.

Feed my fish one more time then set them free with me, not in the reedy river either, hmmmm how about the Nile river?

… Make sure you get my Peace Voices pin and put it on my shirt, it's on my dresser next to my 55 gallon in that silver thing.

Lastly I want you mama to smile and know I put up a great hellified fight.

I just wanna be disowned by God I have no expectations but to rest... I have lived my life struggling with sexuality, wanting my uncles, trying to understand my father, as well as not wanting to lose you.

If I Need to Write A Suicide Note to Mama

Maybe death isn't so bad, and maybe a broken
heart carries a healing secret, and maybe
existence after death is resting and restful.

...

you will hear water echo like rhythms in your
heart, you will chase a spirit that doesn't want to
live on nor can I, so you must rest as I must
rest.

Don't dwell in your heart, it's too big and little
to capacitate worry.

Depression didn't kill me, I would never die by
the hands of anything, depression injured me I
just chose not to heal this time

I heard many voices say, "I like the confusion."

I will be with you every morning
noon
And night.

And tell the Mental Mountains I know it's heights now, I just have not found the key to survival... but it is somewhere in the struggling.

Rebuilding the Temple of Jeremiah

CLINICALLY RESILIENT. A
BIRD BY MOVEMENT

BEATEN BADLY
INTO AN INTELLIGENCE
RESILIENCE

DREAM
YOUTH NEEDS TO SEE
IT'S POSSIBLE

FOLLOW YOURSELF

LOVE AND YOU WILL TEACH
THEM TO FLY

HIT A POINT THAT'S SO ILLEGAL
TO ADVERSITY
IT SENT GOING DOWN BECAUSE
BIRDS FLY
HIGH

Sleep, please show Insomnia how much I need you.

Rebuilding the Temple of Jeremiah

I will be a poem to anyone,
who writes,
who rights and doesn't believe in rights,
I will be a poem to anyone. I will. I promise

Pain Flows

Please.
Anticipation, be my antidepressant,

Flows. Pain voices something, always.

Pain flows and nourishes the fight in me, all the fight I need to be successful, be successful, I am successful.

Rebuilding the Temple of Jeremiah

How are broken, arthritic, tired, journeyed, weathered, bruised, praying, slow healing knees supposed to carry...

A broke, collapsed, big, withdrawn, in tune, dying, crying, revolutionized, traumatized, mentally ill, need to be bleached of impurities heart?
How?

Damn you, damn, you never came
your absence was more supportive.

Damn, you just damned me being the dam
holding me back from seeing what I could really
be... I... could... I could be oceans,

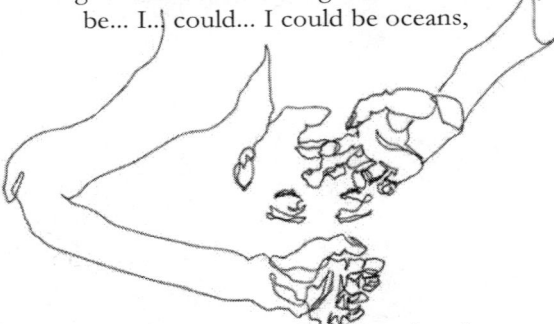

Flooding desserts, you did my raging river a
disservice. I am abundant in knowing I'm a dam
away from being an ocean no one should fuck
with,

I just need to forgive the dam that I let stop me,
the dam that was never there, but there
stopping me, me.

Rebuilding the Temple of Jeremiah

"Acceptance is not easy... but the acceptance of Denial looks stupid and beautifully dangerous."

Did I tell you what Depression did to me,

Did I tell you what Schizophrenia said to me?

They did not want to read my book of life, they wanted to be a part of my final story...

And...

I wanted them to know I am armed and dangerous when writing my chapters!

CEO of My Mind

I want depression to have better posture when fucking with me, sloppy bitch.

If Depression wants me to work for her, she need to sit on top of my mind and run this shit, drive me insane, and take all the credit. Right now she looks like Resilience's bitch.

Don't read my energy, vibes, or face...
Read my lips... fuck you!!

Captivate me, surprise me, bend me bitch.

You can't you only happen in spurts.

The Radiance of Shed Tears for Me and my sister.

"I was never ready to write a poem about the abuse depression took us and us through."
~Jeremiah Davis

"You never know how to be eleven and twelve and adults at the same time" ~Shianna Davis

Sitting in a waiting room for the results of the test depression ran on us...

We qualify...

To suffer.

On the ride to the hospital to see mom... we knew to donate our minds to prayer.

Feeling scared the radiance of our shed tears revealed the way depression did us...

Lock my sister in my room and turnt the lights off...

Whipped my ass because I wanted to sleep...

Rebuilding the Temple of Jeremiah

Made us look our mother in her eyes with expiration in the souls of her eyes... and say "I love you... I need you... but I know I won't always have you."

I have insomnia because I try to figure out who was more of an asshole...

My mama for making us grow and be strong before we could cry for our needs...

Or...

Depression for making us forget us whose innocence belongs to innocence.

We babies in this walking and holding our mothers head blacked out across the floor.

God resurrect our heart, carry us as embryos... innocent of the innocence.

I'm going crazy like depression is going on the hunt....

The radiance of our shed tears...

Show our innocence killed, and our pain our real parents showing us to care for our mother as our child.

And we still cry because our needs unfinished.... kinda like fragmented sentences...

And backs broken from supporting mountains...

And depression being the HBIC

in the bodies of ours.

Rebuilding the Temple of Jeremiah

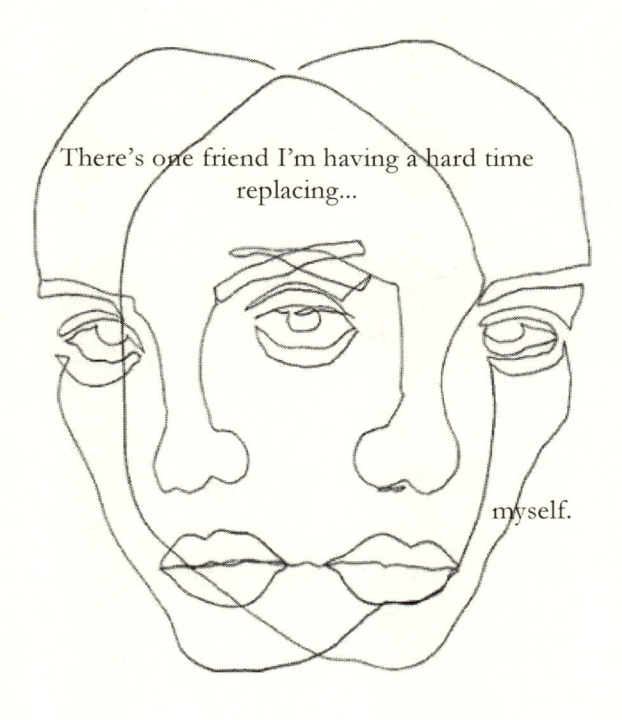

There's one friend I'm having a hard time replacing... myself.

I Don't Wanna Belong

I walk in my depressed room
I get in my depressed bed
I wrap myself in my depressed comforter
I lay on my depressed pillow

And I research Major Depressive Disorder.

I laugh at the symptoms because they're a description of my naked reflection down to my birthmark... sadness.

I see signs that might be a dream come true or a life finally ended... it depends.

I close out the windows of my search, so I can forget the fact my nudes are on the internet... even my birthmark.

I look at my depressed tiger Oscar I forced to be depressed with me, I named her Feisty her

name often gets replaced for Happiness or
Hope because that's what she truly is.

I know when I don't wanna belong she gives
me a reason to wanna stay.

She helps me birth poems and tell poetry the
truth... kinda like this.

Feisty also jumps out the water to kiss my hand,
which makes me feel really special besides my
nudes being on the internet... and my uhh
birthmark.

After I admire the resilience created between
our bond...

I get back in my depressed bed
I wrap myself in my depressed comforter
I lay on my depressed pillow...

And I go to sleep...EVERYDAY... until I have
a doctor's appointment with the therapist.

If Depression Were My Bitch…

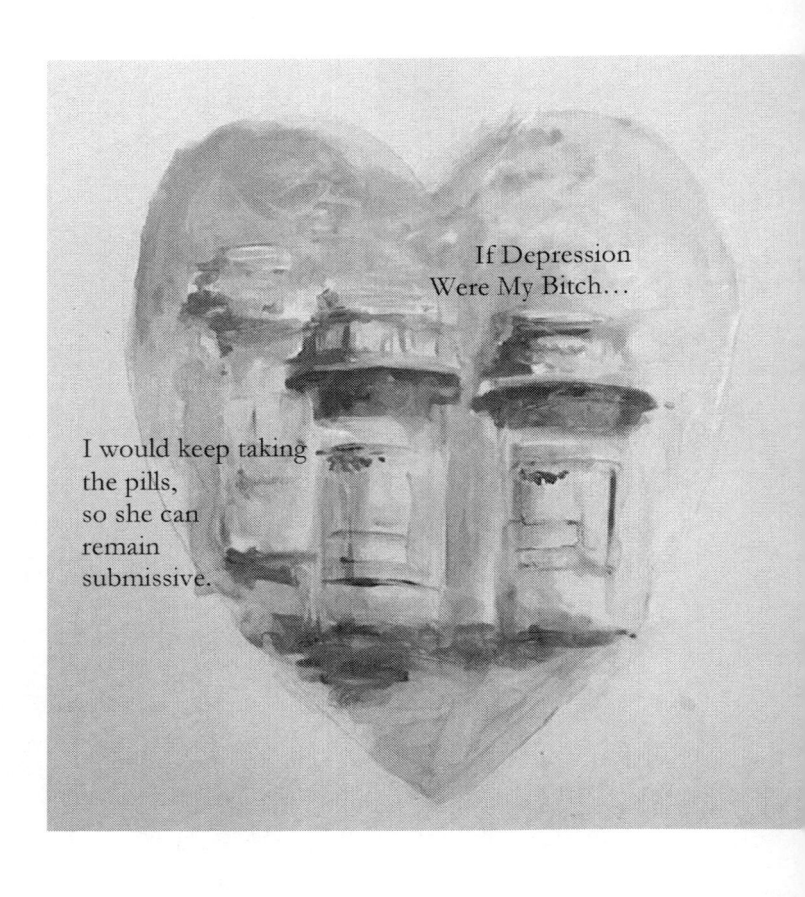

I would keep taking the pills, so she can remain submissive.

Rebuilding the Temple of Jeremiah

Suicide Remarks

Today before I kill this darkness

I... I love, love how much I've been cleaning, hold my ocd responsible.

I just want to say... I wanna say I love the light at the end of the tunnel,

Oh if I could ever reach it.

I hear trauma calling my name and crawling into my shadow.

When I make it to heaven I want God, Jehovah, Jehovah God to know to look at me not the evil, satanic shadow that's attached to my mind.

I love it, I love how much I've cleaned, it's not often these days, not often at all I get to write my feelings as an unstable chaos.

I've cleaned so many scratches from my mind I just have to wait for the pounding of voices in my head to stop.... then........

Signals and Schedule

Fish lights on at night= afraid

Head under covers= hallucinations with voices

Sleep during day= headache from hearing voices

Antsy= fighting characters switch

Pacing= mind ache from everything

Agitation= wanting to do self-harm to keep from harming others

Agitation 2= hate my thoughts

Agitation 3= hate myself for thinking them

Deeeeeeep breathes= fighting HIM!

Silence= whispers in my ear

Rebuilding the Temple of Jeremiah

They don't know...

They don't know what I was reading

If I were reading

They don't know where the idea of these poems come from

If they were ideas

They don't know I'm not fucking kidding with the power of the mind

It will kill me, it wants me dead.

My heart is the resistant.

No Medication

I read a poem

I knew then where my mind needed to go

What I needed to let go and what to dwell on.

I don't need happiness right now, I need
acceptance, let's strive for it.

Knowledge is the riches to have.

I need my books in libraries before I die, not
locked in a computer.

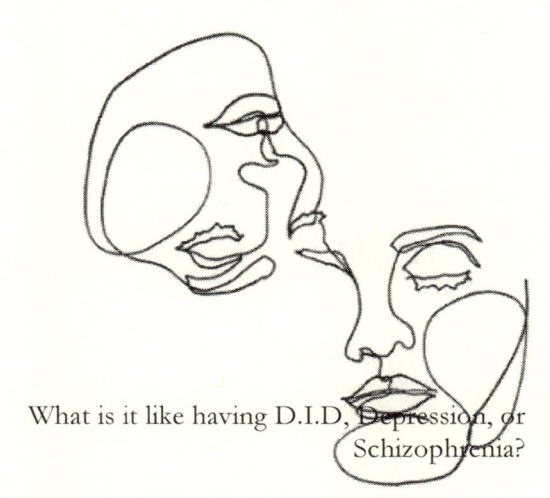

What is it like having D.I.D, Depression, or Schizophrenia?

I'm not sure. I'm just not sure. Some days I don't have neither one, some days I might have all three. There is something that follows me everywhere, every day, a broken mirror with many faces in one reflection. -Jeremiah Davis

To The Mountains

You were everyday hills until we were told otherwise.

We knew how to hike over you minute by minute.

Your deep black ripples of rage
Lifts me up like a chorus.

Your maze is a canvas in which I lose myself painting words that'll get me home.

I lose myself, losing myself in a way I don't want to be found.

I wanna be lost like time but remembered in the final moment.

Can I color your landscape the color of survival

Rebuilding the Temple of Jeremiah

We didn't know we were climbing mountains

We just write to them.

We write to the heart of the mountains.

We lend hindsight to our goal because the mountains...

Were just hills until we were told otherwise.

I can start giving appropriate titles to the right poems.

I love how much I've cleaned

Rebuilding the Temple of Jeremiah

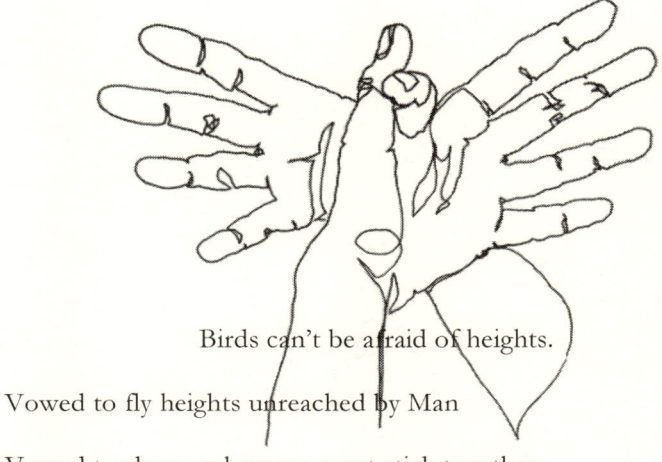

Birds can't be afraid of heights.

Vowed to fly heights unreached by Man

Vowed to show us how we must stick together and realize the ground is a milestone.

Birds make a promise to the ground to never walk when there's a chance to fly, soar, and realize the difference from free and freedom.

Free doesn't cost, freedom is found.

I vow to the bird...

I will find my freedom.

. Undefined Destruction

"How could we just look upon destruction like it could never affect us?" -El Lyrikah

I carry poems, that are tornadoes..
These poems till grounds, bend metal, and breaks hearts.
A young heart swallowing rage like destruction could never affect him.
A young heart watching his mama get murdered by something that can't be convicted.
A innocent tear rocked on a middle finger
"Fuck that little boy" My feelings have heard so many times...
It times like clock work I should get paid to see who gave a fuck about me when my innocence mattered.

"How could we just look upon destruction like it could never affect us?"

Absent bodies for whatever reason simply yell...
We don't give a fuck!

Description of Her

Her lips brewing elixirs of persuasion.

Touch like heavy clouds that carry you until you fall.

I'm only an organism to this Goddess.

Depression has power.

She deceiving as billows of toxic gas to the lungs.

She's a banging rush of cocaine at times I may prefer... just to know I'm not the only substance being abused.

In her eyes carries a universe of lives, and to one, myself she is beautiful.

Today her spirit has power.

Defeat is the success

I don't know how to spell out ocean without the tears.

I know how to fail into something great.

I taste like sweet silky sexy silent striving motivation.

I never got tired of being fat, I got tired of calling myself fat.

Rebuilding the Temple of Jeremiah

                                                          Secretly Gay

Galloping
Against
mYself.

enGraving true
Anatomy
flawlesslY and hidden.

Hurt...ting

3/11/18

I have at least eight uncles, two dads, one
granddad at least
and
They don't know how it feels to be gay,
especially when I don't want to be
and
They don't know me, even when I tell them
and
It hurts
and
Besides your infliction, do you understand?

Rebuilding the Temple of Jeremiah

I'm finally finished with my manuscript for this… and I am still not healed completely…

To be continued.

I'm a bad poet
with hellified lines.
I don't wanna look
godly to God,
I wanna look
like
his imperfect creation.

Rebuilding the Temple of Jeremiah

I refuse to take off my clothes and bend to the
will and desires of someone's sexual fantasies...
I refuse to taint my aura

I am gay. I did not love myself. Not before I confessed this to myself. I am not happy I'm gay. I am confident that I'm insecure. I'm gay.

I'll never know how to tell my father the right way.

I'll never know when.

I'm gay.

I do not accept my sexually satisfying curse.

I'm not a typical gay, I hurt. I long for God to change me before he gets mad and destroys me.

 been gay. is gay. confused.

Tomorrow idk if I'll want a girlfriend, I really don't know.

Rebuilding the Temple of Jeremiah

The biggest mountain right now is the thought of what others will think about me. Not what I think of me. And that's a mountain too, self, value.

If gay were a type of bipolar disorder, because it obviously comes and goes, and flips-flops, with me, is there medication I could take, I don't mind. I just wanna be pleasing to a God I've never seen, never heard, never embraced...

If gay is a problem to my God...

Who am I to love first
a person
I've battled to better
 or a God who never
showed up
at my worst?

You're just watching
my episode of depression.

Yes I am tired.
So tomorrow
 I wanna sleep all day.

Commitment

God I trust you...
 enough to say I love you,
 but because I am in my gay truth
 I can't trust you love me back.

Sincerely,
Broken, torn, ripped, shredded,
depreciated, lost, OCD
about being straight for you,
But I don't know how,
                    Jeremiah

                              Tear... Bucket

Catch all of me.
I am falling and fallen to my own detriment.

Catch all of me.
All of me.
Me…

Rebuilding the Temple of Jeremiah

...

Just me.

Rebuilding the Temple of Jeremiah

Life been happening in waves.
I know not to claim mastery after just the first one.

I can overcome adversity.
I can't overcome not loving myself.

Rebuilding the Temple of Jeremiah

Recognize

If I give you my universe
of thoughts I think you'd abuse me.

Because my universe is flexible... I
can make time look back
on me and wonder my age

I can sweet and swiftly move
the zipper down your pants with just my eyes

I can make you erect seeping
out creative juices begging
me to carry your poetry...

I'm not feeling poetic right now ...
I feel like healing myself by
rejecting your invitation to abuse me.

Laced Vibes

Walk in...

Lights blunt...

Shares secrets...

Grab me by my universe of thoughts,
saying we can be more than friends...

I'm not into sex...
 I wanna see what your mind can do,

Can you look me out of my clothes,
Can you stare down my rage,
Can you rock my imagination,
on you nice,
bulging,
and
 hard opinion of who you think I am...

Who the fuck do you think I am?
... look me in my eyes,
let our eyes lock and kiss intertwining blinks...

Into some sexy shit...

Rebuilding the Temple of Jeremiah

I wanna fuck your mind,

I like the way your mind and
weed jacks off my high...

Stroke my desire,

Make me erect a poem
spelling out what we did and
how we love to fuck with
just a look in each other's eye

How I shoot poems all over the paper about
you... only you...

You.

I want to see your creativity
 make my depression shut the fuck up,
and you hear and listen to what I want...

I want love... I want that shit to start
when I first look you in the eye.

Fuck me with your vision.

                              Heal…ing
I'm trying to heal for the wrong reason.

I want to drink my tears,
Like a cocktail,

Dry my eyes of the oceans.

Can I see perfectly fine, to know?
Where to heal?

Rebuilding the Temple of Jeremiah

Poet to poet

Never ever
Vow to make depression
Smile before yourself.

To my old friend Jeremiah Rashad,

    I didn't know I couldn't live without you, let alone battle these mountains without you. You left me at Suicides will. I promise I'll never wish on you what you did to me and I will always love you enough to rely on myself.
    Sincerely,

Rebuilding the Temple of Jeremiah

                                                                  True Love

Hug me one more time,
My old friend.

We need to part; may I heal us first?

I am sorry for you, neglecting you,
Now I neglect myself.

But I am here now to wipe our tears. I love you
Jeremiah Rashad Davis.
1/13/2007

The mountains are calling me,

Rebuilding the Temple of Jeremiah

to find my lost self

1/13/2007

My year in elementary school I abandoned my future, forget my present, ran from my past, to find nothing but myself living all these years of pain and hurt.

Art Realizes Poetry

Your city of solutions occupied except the
disregarding of you and your excuses.
I'm traveling from my nothing Greenville to
your everything Hollywood where…

Dreams are promoted with reality forgotten.
Molded with your lies I hadda more or less gain
my own truth…
And truth be told I realize you tried to hold
your inauguration of art
In my index of memories but second truth be
told…

Your art (my heart) is my poetry (your mind).

Go and realize the definition of me is the love
of you.
~Jerm

You Needed Me Like

You needed me
Like I need you.

Living trying to heal my past,
Mines.
Forgetting my presence,
Wasting.
Disowning my future,
Not creating.

Stop living what needs to rest.

Rebuilding the Temple of Jeremiah

A Talk to Myself: King Kindly Build Me

Spoke the weight of bricks into these words...
Build me up, from the deserted landfill I am
into a temple of self, and self love.
Mildly aggressively sketch my blueprint.

"Unbreach" my new newborn imperfections,
help, me, help me.

Dictate who I am, raise my imperfections into
something I can kiss on the forehead and say "I
love you" to and love perfectly.

Build me into a better parent and house for my
spirit.
I cannot miss out on who I get to let myself be.
Build me up into a better parent and house for
my spirit,

And just my spirit.

Love At First Compliments

I love you, do I accept you?

I love me do I accept me...
Blown veins,
Veins weakened,
Weakened faith,
Faith tired,
Tired and ready,
Ready for love,
Love find me,
Me find I,
I love you,
Do I accept me?
I love me, I love you,
Do I accept me, I accept you.

Jeremiah you're so beautiful.

To Do List Into I am List

Be confident

Be you

Embrace you

Love who you are

Be who you are

Smile

Do everything you're insecure about

Be everything you're insecure about

Embrace everything you're insecure about

Remember you

Don't hold

Be you

Yes, Be you

You be you

Home is the body

Confident is you

You are empowered

You are confident

This is getting bigger than you

This isn't about you

Think about embracing your flaws to help others embrace themselves

I love you

At the end of haunting

Rebuilding the Temple of Jeremiah

Dear Epistolary Poem,

Tell Jeremiah peace and truth rarely work together, hope and faith compete against each other, reflection and rejection has often started with you. Tell him that the truth about denial is he doesn't have forever to fight that war. He can decide and accept the fate of it to begin to love himself or hate himself and his procrastination. Tell him his struggle to rebuild the man he can be is abundant in inspiring the flames of dark despair. There's no better way to say it, but "living and accepting the truth while trying to remain faithful is haunting." Do it either way. You should be proud of you, you will be proud of you, and I'll always be proud of you.

Sincerely addressed,

Jeremiah D.

God?

God or,

                    Whoever you are,

The one who watches me go through

  hell and compensates with blessings,

                If that's who you are,

Before I lose faith in you,

                I give you everything.

Rebuilding the Temple of Jeremiah

Where can I man up if I'm man down?

I wear the face of misconception.

Floss my identity with strength,

Boost my blood with convulsions from my ego.

I try to comfort outside the comfort of my tears.

Spiritual Pain as Memoir

Does God bless gay people?

When a man of his own depression touched
me, He awakened the "fagget" in me so I've
told myself.

He said unbuckle and unzip my pants as well as
my spiritual beliefs and let him touch my diary
and read my orgasmic body language.

He said I'd love what he did and
till this day I can't help but seek love
 from the synergy he engraved on his hand.

Rebuilding the Temple of Jeremiah

He wrapped his hand around my journey to
explore and began to rise up and compete…

with the power of my God and
come back down making me the
road map to a psychological hell.

At seven years old I never knew
how to not be afraid of the
dark in the day.

At twenty one years old I never knew
how to ask God if he'd grant me peace and
forgiveness because I knew I was a fagget
against my will but I loved the feel and comfort
of a man.

Am I crazy God to like what has broken me,
down to the softest penis after the
climax of shssss don't tell you'll love this?

Am I crazy God because I could advocate
for a broken believer in you, but still love a
man?

Am I crazy God because faith is not my
testimony but pain is my beautiful

attribute to being an understanding human?

Am I going to hell because at seven years old
You did not restore my innocence,
And reverse the damage?

I have a lot of respect for my Heavenly Father
But if that's where I'm going could you join me
For breaking your promise to never leave nor
forsake me?

Rebuilding the Temple of Jeremiah

To be... lived

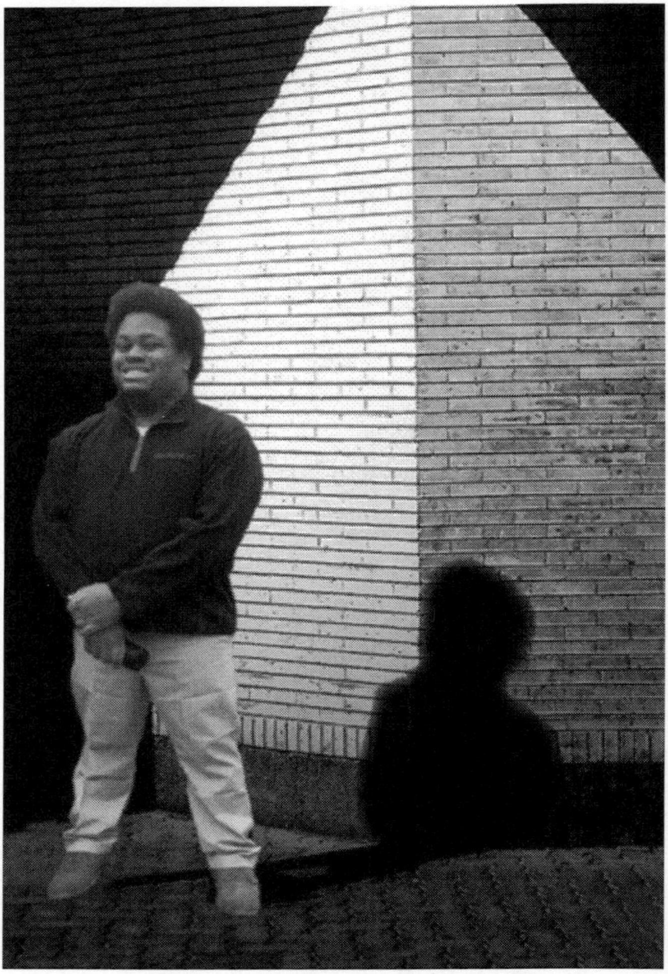

ABOUT THE AUTHOR

Jerm Davitos is a "crazy poet" who refuses to continue to hold back his truths to support his loveable lies. Jeremiah has been writing since 2009. He has been published is several literary journals such as Junto Magazine, The Perch Magazine, editor's choice award from Teen Ink. Being rejected over seventy times, he picks up his pen and ambition seeking the audience that needs his voice. He is interested in revealing the healing in and through his writing of struggles.
Jeremiah also loves a challenge so he forces himself to keep at it, publicly sharing his writing until a life can be changed, will be changed.

Made in the USA
Columbia, SC
31 July 2018